This We Know

This We Know

A Chronology of the Shootings at Kent State,

May 1970

CR

Carole A. Barbato, Laura L. Davis,
and Mark F. Seeman

The Kent State University Press

KENT, OHIO

© 2012 by The Kent State University Press, Kent, Ohio 44242

ALL RIGHTS RESERVED

ISBN 978-1-60635-185-7

Manufactured in the United States of America

LIBRARY OF CONGRESS CATALOGING-IN-PUBLICATION DATA

Barbato, Carole A.

This we know : a chronology of the shootings at Kent State, May 1970 /

Carole A. Barbato, Laura L. Davis, and Mark F. Seeman.

pages cm

ISBN 978-1-60635-185-7 (pbk.) ∞

1. Kent State Shootings, Kent, Ohio, 1970.

2. Student movements—Ohio—Kent—History—20th century.

I. Title.

LD4191.O72B37 2012

378.771'37—dc23

2012048061

19 18 17 16 15   5 4 3

For Sandy, Bill, Allison, and Jeff

Contents

Preface

What happened on May 4, 1970? It is a story that continues to be written. Still, we have documented facts that fill out the chronology of the events at Kent State—the four days in May that ended with members of the Ohio National Guard wounding nine Kent State students and fatally shooting Sandra Scheuer, Jeffrey Miller, Allison Krause, and William Schroeder. *This We Know* gathers well-established information from recorded accounts—from the time they happened through what we have learned since.

While many know generally what happened, they are often surprised by the details. It is not a story in which what you think happened necessarily is what did happen. Common sense and logic do not fully explain the sequence. Think back to Philosophy 101 or *The West Wing* episode titled "Post Hoc, Ergo Propter Hoc." The Latin phrase reveals the fallacy: Since this event occurred *after* that one, this event must have been caused by that one. Resisting the fallacy, we must remember that the dramatic events of May 1, 2, and 3 preceded May 4, but did not cause what happened on May 4. Windows were broken on Friday. A building burned on Saturday. A sit-in was staged on Sunday. However, these events did not cause guardsmen to fire their rifles on Monday.

As you find your path to historical understanding, words written by Allison Krause might provide a guide. On a history exam in 1970, she wrote: "Dates and facts are not enough to show what happened in the past. It is necessary to delve into the human side of history to come up with the truth. History must be made relevant to the present to make it useful." Why did the Guard shoot on May 4, 1970, ending Allison's life and the lives of Bill, Sandy, and Jeff? Is that story relevant to you?

The Kent State University May 4 Visitors Center offers you the dates and facts of *This We Know* as an entrée to understanding what happened in the past. Walk through that door to delve into the human side of history in the May 4 Visitors Center. Experience the struggle for social justice and generational divides that stood as a backdrop for the shootings at Kent State. Immerse yourself in what happened on May 4. Witness the worldwide impact of the event. Reflect on whether this history is of use today to help preserve the principles of democratic societies.

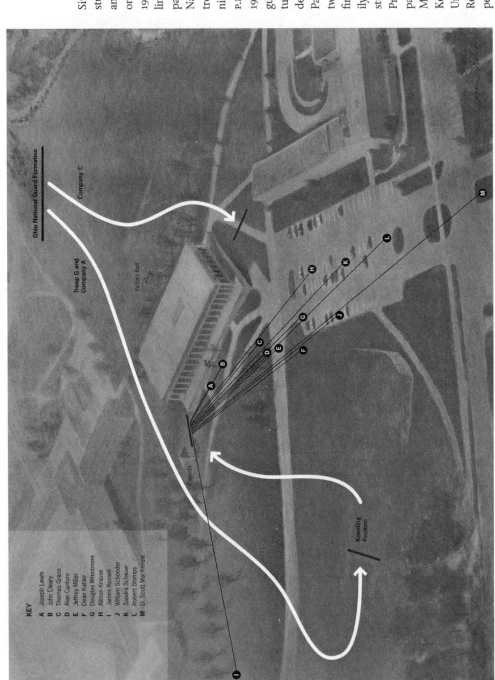

Site of the student rally and shootings on May 4, 1970. Curved lines trace the path of Ohio National Guard troops beginning at 12:05 P.M. on May 4, 1970. At 12:24, guardsmen turned 135 degrees at the Pagoda and twenty-eight, primarily toward students in the Prentice Hall parking lot. Map copyright Kent State University. Reprinted with permission.

KEY

A Joseph Lewis
B John Cleary
C Thomas Grace
D Alan Canfora
E Jeffrey Miller
F Dean Kahler
G Douglas Wrentmore
H Allison Krause
I James Russell
J William Schroeder
K Sandra Scheuer
L Robert Stamps
M D. Scott MacKenzie

Ohio National Guard Formation

Company C

Troop G and Company A

Victory Bell

Pagoda

Kneeling Position

This We Know

I have concluded that the actions of the enemy in the last 10 days clearly endanger the lives of Americans who are in Vietnam now and would constitute an unacceptable risk to those who will be there after withdrawal of another 150,000. To protect our men who are in Vietnam, and to guarantee the continued success of our withdrawal and Vietnamization program, I have concluded that the time has come for action. . . . We take this action not for the purpose of expanding the war into Cambodia but for the purpose of ending the war in Vietnam and winning the just peace we all desire.[1]

These words, spoken by President Richard M. Nixon on Thursday, April 30, 1970, at 9:00 P.M., represented to many an escalation of the war in Vietnam, not the de-escalation he had promised since 1968. The invasion of Cambodia was seen by many as a betrayal, "a cataclysmic move that turned the War in Vietnam into the War in Indochina."[2] As social justice advocate Peter Davies noted, "The groans on numerous campuses that night turned into impassioned and sometimes violent protests the next day." According to the analysis of political sociologist Seymour Lipset, "The reaction against the May 1970 Cambodian incursion, of course, produced the largest and most extensive student protest movement the United States has ever experienced. All the survey data document the increased extent of student participation, as well as the fact that student attitudes in general moved to the Left, not only with respect to the war, but on other issues as well."[3]

FRIDAY, MAY 1, 1970

On Friday, May 1, 1970, students at Kent State University, like thousands of others at hundreds of colleges and universities throughout the United States, participated in a protest against the U.S. invasion of Cambodia. While protests at some other colleges and universities were violent, this rally was impassioned but peaceful.

Kent State history graduate students Steve Sharoff and Chris Plant awoke early in the morning to plan a campus protest against Nixon's announcement of the incursion into Cambodia. By 7:00 A.M., they were distributing flyers announcing a rally at noon.[4] At noon, about five hundred students gathered at the Commons, a grassy green in the center of campus.[5] A group that called itself WHORE (World Historians Opposed to Racism and Exploitation) ceremonially buried a copy of the Constitution. According to "The Justice Department's Summary of FBI Reports" on the shootings, "The general theme of the speeches was that the President had disregarded the limits of his office imposed by the Constitution of the United States and that, as a consequence, the Constitution had become a lifeless document, murdered by the President."[6] Someone burned his draft card, and veteran James Geary, another history graduate student who had won the Silver Star for his service in Vietnam, burned his discharge papers in protest against the invasion of Cambodia.[7] Those present agreed to meet at noon on Monday, May 4, to determine if they should join other universities and colleges throughout America in a national student strike. The assembly began and ended peacefully.

Later that afternoon, Kent State's Black United Students (BUS) held a rally on front campus to hear a speaker from Ohio State University talk about violence by law enforcement officials during demonstrations there. Black students advised their peers to stay away from campus activities that weekend. The short, forty-five-minute meeting disbanded peacefully. Upon hearing of the two peaceful protests, KSU's president, Robert I. White, left for Iowa, where he was to sit on the American College Testing board of trustees meeting on Sunday and take some time while there to visit with family.[8]

On Friday, May 1, Kent State students protest the invasion of Cambodia by symbolically burying a copy of the U.S. Constitution at the Victory Bell on the Commons. Reprinted with permission of Kent State University Special Collections and Archives.

Friday evening was "one of the first warm Friday nights of the spring."[9] The small city of Kent had a strip of bars and clubs in the downtown area on North Water Street that attracted young people (students and nonstudents) from all over the state and the local area. Friday night was no exception. Thousands of young people were in the bars and clubs. Between 10:00 and 11:00 P.M., firecrackers were set off and a motorcycle gang called the Chosen Few was riding up and down Water Street between two bars, JB's and the Kove, performing tricks on their bikes. A police car drove past the crowd four or five times and was met with cheers as it drove by.[10] The *Report of the President's Commission on Campus Unrest* stated that ten police officers were on duty that evening, and four of these men in two patrol cars were assigned to North Water Street.[11] A trash can was dumped in the middle of Water Street, stopping the flow of traffic north and south. People danced in the street, preventing cars from passing through. Around 11:20 P.M., some members of the crowd hit the passing police car with beer bottles. According to Davies, members of the Chosen Few lit the contents of the trash can, causing a small fire in the middle of Water Street.[12] It was described by some as a "bonfire," but it was a rather small trash fire.[13]

The *Akron Beacon Journal* Special Report noted that "Patrolman Robert Defluiter of the Kent Police Department said that between 11:27 and 11:41 P.M. he watched young demonstrators shouting 'Get out of town, pigs!' bombard two police cars with bottles, glasses and beer pitchers."[14] Many people who were in the bars came up to see what was going on and to escape the heat inside. "Soon the crowd blocked the street and began to stop motorists to ask their opinion about Cambodia."[15] The crowd turned revelry to an antiwar protest. According to the Justice Department's Summary, at 11:41 P.M. all of Kent's twenty-one police officers were summoned to duty. The nearby Stow Police Department was alerted, as well as the Portage County Sheriff Department, which sent eighty to ninety regular and special deputies to Kent. Kent police and sheriff's deputies began marching down Water Street. One squad formed at Main and Water, and the other marched down North Water Street to break up the revelry near the trash fire. The crowd, now around four hundred to five hundred in number according to the Justice Department's Summary, began running ahead of the police.[16] Davies noted that about twenty people started throwing bottles at buildings.[17] Within the city of Kent, forty-seven windows were broken in fifteen buildings.[18]

After consulting with Kent's police chief, Roy Thompson, Mayor Leroy Satrom declared a state of civil emergency at 12:20 A.M. and ordered all bars to be closed. He set a curfew of 11:00 P.M. for the city and 1:00 A.M. for the campus. Thompson and the Kent police enforced this order.[19] This action sent hundreds more young people into the streets and into the middle of the protesters, tear gas, and police action. Soon bystanders were being caught up in the crowd. At 12:47 A.M., Mayor Satrom called the office of Ohio's governor, James Rhodes, informing him that the SDS (Students for a

Democratic Society) had taken over part of the city of Kent. In fact, the KSU chapter of the SDS had been disbanded in the spring of 1969. The governor's administrative assistant, John McElroy, called Maj. Gen. Sylvester Del Corso of the Ohio National Guard, who called the Guard liaison officer, Lieutenant Charles Barnette.[20]

Some of the crowd from downtown were forced onto campus, where they were safe from police action. When a traffic accident left an electric worker stranded—hanging on the traffic light at the corner of Lincoln and Main (the entrance to the Kent State campus)—police and members of the crowd on the campus grounds worked together to assist the worker to safety.[21] By 2:00 A.M., the streets of downtown Kent were cleared of all people; police arrested fifteen, all from Ohio—"not an unusually large number for a weekend evening in downtown Kent."[22] Although, according to the Justice Department's Summary, the mayor originally estimated that the disorder had caused damage to the downtown area worth $50,000 (later revising this figure to $15,000), the final figure was an estimated $10,000.[23]

Lieutenant Charles Barnette of the Ohio National Guard arrived at the city of Kent to talk with the mayor at 2:27 A.M. James Best, a Kent State political science professor, concluded, "Frustration over the Cambodian invasion, anger because they were turned out of bars, and the sting of tear gas turned what might have otherwise been a relatively harmless release of emotion into an ugly incident."[24] According to the *Report of the President's Commission,* "University Police Chief Donald L. Schwartzmiller had decided to use his men to guard campus buildings. That night, a small amount of property damage, including a broken window at the ROTC building, was done on campus." The commission concluded, "The pattern established on Friday night was to recur throughout the weekend: There were disorderly incidents; authorities could not or did not respond in time to apprehend those responsible to stop the incidents in their early stages; the disorder grew; the police action, when it came, involved bystanders as well as participants; and finally, the students drew together in the conviction that they were being arbitrarily harassed."[25]

SATURDAY, MAY 2, 1970

Saturday morning began with some students assisting shop owners in cleaning up the glass from the windows broken in the stores the evening before. Sightseers examined the damage. Owners of the stores and townspeople called City Hall, demanding that something be done. The mayor and the city chief of police were convinced that the SDS Weathermen were in the area and blamed them for the destruction in downtown Kent as part of a radical plot. Conversely, KSU's police chief, Donald Schwartzmiller, later commented that the campus police did not have any information about the Weathermen being at Kent State that weekend. He noted that the city police must have seen something his own force had not.[26] According to the *Akron Beacon Journal*, "To paraphrase Voltaire's remark about God, if Weatherman did not exist, it would have to be invented. Weatherman, the most militant wing of the SDS, seems to have become a kind of policeman's shorthand for anyone who is bearded, surly and inclined toward violence."[27]

Officials met several times throughout the day. The mayor formally proclaimed a civil emergency, banning all sales of liquor, beer, firearms, and gasoline (unless it was pumped directly into a car or truck). He declared an 8:00 P.M. to 6:00 A.M. curfew for the city and the university. A meeting of the mayor, KSU officials, and Lieutenant Barnette, the Guard liaison, determined that the curfew on campus would be 1:00 A.M. At 1:00 P.M., in a meeting of Lieutenant Barnette and Vice President Robert Matson from the university, it was agreed that if arrests were to be conducted on campus, the university would first call on its campus police, second the sheriff's department, and third the Ohio State Highway Patrol. Lieutenant Barnette warned that if the National Guard was called to assist, they would not make a distinction between the city of Kent and the university.[28] According to Lieutenant Col. Charles Fassinger, however, the role of the National Guard was to assist officials and not take over for other police enforcing agencies.[29] Lieutenant Barnette told Mayor Satrom that if he planned to request the services of the Guard, he must do so by 5:00 P.M. that day (Saturday). The Ohio National Guard already was mobilized at the time and stationed in the nearby city of Akron, because of threats and disorder associated with a Teamsters Union wildcat strike there.

For several reasons, Satrom met the Guard deadline: rumors of radical SDS involvement from outside the area, reports by shop owners of threats, a decision of the sheriff's office and campus police not to assist the city, and the availability of the Highway Patrol only for making arrests. The mayor asked for the Guard to be put on alert in the city to protect citizens and property, and Governor Rhodes authorized the troops' dispatch to Kent. The National Guard was called up and moved to Kent at 6:00 P.M.[30]

Although civil emergency and an 8:00 P.M. curfew were in effect in the city of Kent, the curfew on Kent State's campus was set at 1:00 A.M. KSU Vice President Matson met with undergraduate student leaders to plan evening activities on campus. They sent leaflets to the dorms to announce the curfew in the city and the plans for dormitory dances and bands, and, specifically, to state that peaceful assemblies were *not banned* on campus.[31]

Rumors circulated among officials in the city and the university that the campus's Reserve Officers' Training Corps (ROTC) building would be a target.[32] By 7:00 P.M., a crowd started to form on the Commons near the Victory Bell; by 7:30 P.M., it numbered six hundred.[33] The campus police were not guarding the ROTC building, as they had the evening before when Kent State student Michael Weekly broke one of its windows. Weekly was the only one charged with doing any damage to the ROTC building that weekend.[34]

The *Report of the President's Commission* noted that KSU Police Chief Schwartz-miller called the Highway Patrol for assistance but was notified that it would come only if arrests were necessary. Since at this time the assembly was peaceful and lawful and no arrests were warranted, the Patrol was not called back. The KSU police did not go to the ROTC building at this time either.[35]

Faculty marshals wearing either blue or white armbands circulated throughout the crowd, distributing leaflets notifying participants of the 1:00 A.M. campus curfew and announcing a rumor control telephone number.[36] The crowd marched from the Commons past the dormitories, picking up more students and nonstudents as it marched around campus until its numbers had grown to between one thousand and two thousand people.[37] The *Report of the President's Commission* stated that "some were chanting, 'Ho, Ho, Ho Chi Minh,' and 'One, two, three, four, we don't want your fucking war.' As they crossed the Commons near the ROTC building, some shouted, 'Get it,' 'Burn it,' and 'ROTC has to go.'"[38] According to the Justice Department's Summary, "The wooden ROTC building, a target for some students because of its symbolism of U.S. involvement in Southeast Asia, was located on the western portion of the Commons. It became the focal point of the demonstration."[39] At 8:10 P.M., a few members of the crowd began throwing rocks at the ROTC build-ing, breaking more windows. Although others threw railroad flares, they rolled off without setting it on fire. A male dipped a rag into a motorcycle gas tank and tried to set the curtains on fire, and, after thirty minutes and many failed attempts, the building started to burn. Approximately one dozen members of the crowd actively tried to set the building on fire.[40] According to the FBI report, the building was afire by 8:30 P.M., but the fire department was not notified until 8:49 P.M., when it sent trucks to the scene. Mayor Satrom, notified of the trouble on campus, called out the Ohio National Guard without conferring with university officials.[41]

At 9:00 P.M., the Kent City Fire Department arrived to put out the ROTC fire, unescorted by police. The firefighters were met with jeers and resistance from the demonstrators, several of whom threw rocks, tried to cut the fire hoses, or pulled on the hoses in a tug-of-war.[42] At 9:15 P.M., just as the firefighters were leaving, the KSU police arrived at the scene. The university police used tear gas to disperse the crowd, which scattered. At this point, by all reports, the fire was out.[43] The KSU police were joined by ten officers from the Portage County Sheriff's Office.[44] Around 9:30 P.M., a small supply shed on the edge of the Commons, near the tennis courts, was set on fire, and some of the faculty marshals and students formed a makeshift bucket brigade to put out the fire and save a nearby tree.[45] The remaining students were dispersed by officers of the university police and sheriff's department. University officials called the Ohio State Highway Patrol, which was already on campus, stationed at President

On the evening of Saturday, May 2, Ohio National Guard troops enter the Kent State campus when the ROTC building burns. Photo copyright Don Roese, *Akron Beacon Journal.* Reprinted with permission.

White's residence. Around 9:45 P.M., the fire at the ROTC building, which had been unattended by the firefighters, flared back up and burned "furiously," according to the Justice Department's Summary.[46] Although it is widely assumed that the building was burned by demonstrators, it also has been suggested by some researchers that the arson was the work of agents provocateurs.[47]

At 10:10 P.M., firefighters were dispatched a second time to the ROTC building, accompanied this time by the Ohio National Guard. According to the Justice Department's Summary, the guardsmen sent to the vicinity of the ROTC building belonged to the Ohio National Guard's Company A and Troop G. As Troop G approached campus, its vehicles were hit by rocks. Eight guardsmen reported injuries; one required medical attention.[48] Demonstrators who returned to the ROTC building found it fully engulfed in flames. By now, although the university police, sheriff's deputies, highway patrolmen, and guardsmen were helping the firefighters, the small, wooden, World War II barracks building could not be saved. From this point until midnight, the National Guard drove demonstrators into the dorms even if they were not residents of those dorms. Faculty marshals also got swept up in this action. According to the *Report of the President's Commission,* when faculty marshals tried to approach guardsmen to explain who they were, the guardsmen knelt down and raised their rifles. At this point, the faculty gave up trying to reason with the guardsmen and just ran away from them. The report further noted, "Neither Del Corso nor Canterbury requested permission of any university official before sending troops onto campus. General Canterbury said later that because the building was located on state property, the Guard needed no specific invitation to enter the campus."[49]

Sunday, May 3, 1970

On Sunday, May 3, students who lived on campus awoke to see 850 guardsmen occupying the grounds.[50] Some troops guarded the site of the ROTC building and set up camp on the football field (now the Kent Student Center parking lot). Guardsmen were posted throughout the campus with bayoneted and loaded rifles. Students were not informed, and most did not suspect, that the rifles were loaded.

At 9:00 A.M., Governor Rhodes flew into Kent by helicopter from Cleveland, Ohio, where he had been campaigning for the U.S. Senate primary election. He viewed damages in the city and on campus and met with officials at the city fire station. These officials included the Portage County prosecutor, Ronald Kane; Major General Del Corso of the Ohio National Guard; three university officials; and representatives from the State Highway Patrol and the Portage County Sheriff's Office. After a brief private discussion, the governor opened the meeting to the press and delivered a fifteen-minute law-and-order speech.[51] Thumping his fist on the table, he proclaimed that Kent State was just one of many Ohio universities being taken over by those trying to attack authority and use the universities as sanctuaries and said that officials would use any means necessary to control them. He called the disturbances at Kent State "probably the most vicious form of campus-oriented violence yet perpetuated by dissident groups and their allies in the state of Ohio." Then he added, "They're worse than the 'Brown Shirt' [sic] and the communist element and also the 'night riders' and the Vigilantes. They're the worst type of people that we harbor in America. And I want to say that they're not going to take over the campus. And the campus now is going to be part of the County and the State of Ohio. There is no sanctuary for these people to burn buildings down of private citizens—of businesses in a community and then run into a sanctuary. It is over with in Ohio."[52] Guardsmen stationed on campus and others in the area heard the broadcasted speech. Some agreed with Rhodes's rhetoric. Others felt the remarks were deliberately inflammatory and believed that they did in fact have a volatile effect on the situation. Many people, including university officials, interpreted the governor's statements to mean that Kent State was under martial law. However,

Rhodes never did call for a state of emergency, "and indeed, Governor Rhodes's order committing the Ohio National Guard to the town of Kent, and the campus, did not become official until May 5, the day after the thirteen students were shot."[53] According to a report in *Kent* magazine, Portage County's prosecutor wanted the governor to close the university until things calmed down, but Rhodes refused to do so, saying it "would be playing into the hands of the SDS and the Weathermen."[54]

As noted earlier, Governor Rhodes was running in the Republican primary for a U.S. Senate seat, competing against a very popular candidate, Robert Taft. Since Rhodes was running on a law-and-order platform, KSU's President White, now home from his trip to Iowa, assumed that the governor was going to seek the state of emergency that would invoke martial law and believed that the National Guard was in control of the campus. With Rhodes's visit, even without the declaration of a state of emergency, the role of the National Guard changed from protecting property and assisting local law enforcement officials to one of breaking up any assembly on campus, peaceful or otherwise.[55]

Robert Matson, KSU's vice president for student affairs, and the student body president, Frank Frisina, distributed the second leaflet of that weekend. Unlike the first, this leaflet proclaimed a ban on all rallies. Few students saw the leaflets. Meanwhile, because so many people were flocking to the Kent State campus to see the burned building, all sightseers were banned from the campus by 1:00 P.M. on Sunday.[56]

By 7:00 P.M., a crowd had again gathered at the Victory Bell on the Commons, and by 8:45 P.M., it had grown so large that university officials moved up a curfew from 1:00 A.M. to 9:00 P.M. Students surveyed after the shootings reported that their motivation for attending the Sunday rally was to protest the occupation of their campus by the Ohio National Guard.[57] According to the Justice Department's Summary, around 9:15 P.M., a member of the university police ordered the crowd on the Commons to disperse, telling demonstrators if they did not they would be subject to arrest. The group did not disperse, but after being teargassed, it split into two directions. One group of people headed for President White's house, and the other group headed in the opposite direction, toward the gate at Lincoln and Main streets leading to town. Those who moved toward the president's house were gassed by guardsmen and retreated back to the Commons area, when some went to join the other group at Lincoln and Main. This second group conducted a sit-in in the intersection of Lincoln and Main streets, blocking traffic in all directions.[58] "About 200 students sat down in the street there," reported the *Akron Beacon Journal*, "backed by about 500 others on the campus behind them. . . . The students sang 'Give Peace a Chance,' while a military helicopter with a searchlight circled overhead."[59] According to the Justice Department's Summary, "Law enforcement officers from the city and county faced the students while National Guardsmen took a position

behind them. State police helicopters were overhead with searchlights being played on the crowd."[60]

At 10:10 P.M., sit-in demonstrators sought to discuss six demands with Mayor Satrom and KSU's President White: abolition of the ROTC program, removal of the National Guard from campus by Monday night, the lifting of the curfew, full amnesty for those arrested Saturday night, consideration for the demands of BUS, and a reduction in tuition. When a student used a bullhorn to read these demands aloud, the sit-in participants greeted each with cheers. One student (it is not clear whether this was the same student who read these demands) talked with police officials and then announced to the crowd that "the National Guard would be immediately leaving the front Campus . . . in response to their demands that they speak with Mayor Satrom, President White, and/or Governor Rhodes."[61]

Thinking that an agreement had been reached, sit-in participants began moving out of the intersection. Only after they had done so, the National Guard announced over a loudspeaker that the curfew had been moved up from 1:00 A.M. to 11:00 P.M. and that the crowd should disperse immediately. The demonstrators felt betrayed; some yelled obscenities and threw rocks. The guardsmen threw tear gas and advanced on the crowd, using their bayonets to break it up. About two hundred students attempted to escape into nearby Rockwell Hall, which housed the library. Two students reported being bayoneted at this time, and students were held captive in this building for about forty-five minutes.[62] Later, remaining students in the library were peacefully removed by the Ohio State Highway Patrol. The other group of three hundred students was pursued by guardsmen across campus to the Tri-Towers dormitory complex, where it was teargassed.[63] A total of sixty-eight demonstrators was arrested for curfew violation and failure to disperse.[64] According to Davies, fifty-one students were arrested for curfew violations.[65] The *Akron Beacon Journal* reported, "The first two student injuries occurred on this Sunday night—Helen Opaskar, 21, of Cleveland, and Joell Richardson, 19, of Sterling, N.Y., both pricked by Guardsmen's bayonets."[66] Anecdotal evidence suggests that additional students were bayoneted but did not report their injuries. The campus was noisy and hectic during the rest of the night, as helicopters hovered overhead shining searchlights below; some students were caught unable to return to their dormitories because of the hurriedly imposed curfew.[67]

Facing page: On the evening of Sunday, May 3, students sit in at the intersection of Lincoln and Main to protest the presence of the National Guard on campus. Photo copyright *Akron Beacon Journal.* Reprinted with permission.

The approximately twenty thousand Kent campus students arose that sunny but brisk spring morning ready to attend their classes as usual—but there would prove to be nothing usual about the day. Morning classes began with somewhat higher than typical student absenteeism, but with a "superficial appearance of normality."[68] Several fake bomb threats (a fairly common prank) caused several classes to be canceled and one classroom building to be evacuated. Quite uncommon, Ohio National Guardsmen stood at their posts throughout campus in full gear, with bayoneted rifles, guarding the entrances to the campus, its buildings, and the remains of the ROTC building on the Commons. Their presence shocked and angered some students, especially those who, having spent the weekend at their homes or off-campus residences, were seeing the guardsmen for the first time. President White met with his cabinet at 7:00 A.M. and with the Executive Committee of the Faculty Senate at 8:00 A.M., agreeing at the latter meeting to call together the full faculty to discuss the situation on campus.[69]

At 10:00 A.M., a meeting was called by Gen. Canterbury of the Ohio National Guard. Attending it were President White and Vice President Matson representing the university; the Guard legal officer, Maj. William R. Shimp; Mayor Satrom, the police chief, Roy Thompson, and the police safety director, Paul Hershey, representing the city of Kent; and Maj. Donald E. Manly of the Ohio State Highway Patrol.[70] Because the separate curfew hours set for the city of Kent and the university were causing some confusion, those meeting decided to set a uniform curfew running from 8:00 P.M. to 6 A.M. for both. The officials raised other matters as well. General Canterbury stated his desire to withdraw his troops as soon as possible, perhaps as early as that evening. The rally scheduled for noon on the KSU campus also was discussed, although the course of the discussion was described differently in the testimony given before the President's Commission on Campus Unrest and in the courtroom trials. For example, Canterbury testified that he first learned about the rally at this morning meeting, adding that when he asked President White if it should be banned, White said it should be. President White refuted Canterbury's account, however, commenting, "From past history, all know that my response would have been affirmative to a rally." Other participants likewise disagreed over what was said at the meeting. Some did not recall President White agreeing that the rally should be banned, but in the end they did come away thinking that the rally was banned.[71] This confusion over the planned rally extended to the campus at large. Some weren't sure if any additional rallies would be legal. Nevertheless, word spread that the rally would be held on the Commons at noon, as had been planned since May 1.

It should be noted again that although Mayor Satrom had declared a civil emergency on May 2, 1970, and troops had been called in to assist civil authority, no one had sought or obtained the injunction required for a state of emergency by noon on May 4. The extent to which the prerogatives granted the ONG within the city of Kent, as negotiated between Mayor Satrom and Major General Del Corso, would extend to the university campus likewise remained unclear; at the time, a statement by Maj. Harry Jones that the National Guard was legally empowered to forbid public gatherings on campus was accepted as truth.[72] Based on this discussion, the university prepared and distributed leaflets to students for the second time that weekend. "The leaflet listed curfew hours; said the governor through the National Guard had assumed legal control of the campus; stated that all outdoor demonstrations and rallies, peaceful or otherwise, were prohibited by the state of emergency; and said the Guard was empowered to make arrests."[73] Only the curfew hours were technically correct. In any case, many of the students were unaware of these directives either because they lived off campus and didn't receive them or because they didn't retrieve and read the leaflets from their student mailboxes until after the shootings. Other students simply disregarded them.[74]

The Victory Bell began tolling around 11:00 A.M., summoning people to the rally on the Commons. At about 11:30 A.M., General Canterbury arrived at the campus Administration Building, in which the National Guard was headquartered. Upon entering the building, he stated that the rally on the Commons was banned. "Major John Simons, chaplain of the 107th Armored Cavalry Regiment, expressed concern that the students might be unaware that the noon rally had been prohibited. He [Canterbury] said a campus official told him that the university radio station would 'spread the word.'" General Canterbury, who did not have time to change into his uniform, and Lieutenant Col. Charles Fassinger, the highest-ranked uniformed officer reporting to the Commons, arrived there between 11:30 A.M. and 11:49 A.M. They saw the crowd grow from about five hundred students to about two thousand by noon.[75] The Justice Department's Summary estimated that two hundred to three hundred students had gathered near the Victory Bell, with another one thousand or so behind them on the hill.[76] By 11:45 A.M., 113 ONG troops and officers took position around the site of the ROTC building at the northern edge of the Commons, 51 from Company A, 36 from Company C, and 16 from Troop G, together led by 10 officers, including General Canterbury, Lieutenant Colonel Fassinger, and Major Jones.[77] Fassinger ordered the troops to form a line near the ROTC site. Troops locked and loaded their weapons if they hadn't already done so.[78]

At the time the rally was beginning, morning classes were ending. Many students were breaking for lunch or returning to their dorms. The student union known as the Hub, a place where students could go for lunch or to talk and relax between classes, was adjacent to the Commons and near the ROTC building. Because the Commons was the central intersection and heartbeat of the campus, the crowd there grew quickly. The lie of the land encouraged onlookers as well: "The hills made a

natural amphitheater from which students could watch events on the Commons floor."[79] The motivations of those attending the rally varied: some were protesting the continuing presence of the National Guard and its treatment of students on *their* college campus; some were continuing the protest over U.S. policy begun on Friday after President Nixon announced the incursion into Cambodia; others were curious spectators or were simply passersby, crossing the Commons on their way to and from class. Faculty marshals were present at the site of this Monday rally, as they had been during the previous few days. However, as faculty marshal Ken Calkins commented, they "had been reduced essentially to the status of mere spectators . . . watch[ing] powerlessly" as the Guard took action.[80]

At 11:45 A.M., as the National Guard formed up near the ROTC building, the students were gathered around the Victory Bell, five hundred feet away. By all accounts, the assembly was peaceful.[81]

General Canterbury ordered the demonstrators to leave the Commons, but because of the noise and the distance, his order was not heard. KSU police officer Harold Rice used a bullhorn to relay the general's order for the crowd to disperse. Many students probably still did not hear the order, or if they did, they did not disperse. Next, Rice crossed the Commons in a jeep, accompanied by two guardsmen, "who rode 'shotgun' in the rear seat." Once again, Rice used the bullhorn to announce, "This assembly is unlawful. The crowd must disperse at this time. This is an order!"[82] The jeep was met with shouts and jeers by the demonstrators, some chanting, "Pigs off our campus!" "1, 2, 3, 4. We don't want your fucking war," "Power to the people," and "Strike, Strike, Strike."[83] Some demonstrators threw rocks. One bounced off a tire on the jeep. When the jeep returned to the line of guardsmen near the ROTC ruins, the students cheered, and several made unfavorable gestures at the guardsmen. While the crowd remained in place at the Victory Bell, Rice and the guardsmen approached two more times in the jeep, and each time they returned to the line their retreat was met with jeers and cheers by the students. The third time, Major Jones ran out to the jeep and ordered it to return to the skirmish line at the northwestern corner of the Commons.[84]

The dispersal announcement was ineffectual in banning the peaceful rally. General Canterbury next gave the order to shoot tear gas into the crowd to disband it. Lieutenant Colonel Fassinger ordered eight to ten grenadiers with M-79 grenade launchers to fire two volleys of tear gas into the crowd. While this did prompt some students to scatter and retreat slightly up Blanket Hill toward Taylor Hall, most remained. Some of the tear gas canisters had fallen short because of poor aim

Facing page: At 11:45 A.M. on Monday, May 4, guardsmen line up 500 feet away from the student rally at the Victory Bell on the Commons. Reprinted with permission of Kent State University Special Collections and Archives.

As officers issue an order to disperse to demonstrators, other students continue to pass through this hub of the campus on their way to class. Photo copyright Richard Kevern. Reprinted with permission.

and the fifteen-mile-per-hour winds that were blowing to the southwest. However, students threw a few of the canisters back toward the line of guardsmen, raising cheers and causing some in the crowd to chant, "Pigs off campus."[85]

At this point, another announcement was made over a loudspeaker for all to disperse. The demonstrators responded with chants and jeers. According to the *Report of the President's Commission*, "Many students felt that the campus was their 'turf.' Unclear about the authority vested in the Guard by the governor, or indifferent to it, some also felt that their constitutional right to free assembly was being infringed upon. As they saw it, they had been ordered to disperse at a time when no rocks had been thrown and no other violence had been committed. Many told interviewers later, 'We weren't doing anything.'"[86]

At approximately 12:05 p.m., General Canterbury ordered the troops to advance on the demonstrators. Thirty Ohio state highway patrolmen stayed on the Commons, ready to make any necessary arrests.[87] As reported in Michener and in testimony to a federal grand jury, Canterbury said, "These students . . . are going to have to find out what law and order is all about."[88] Guardsmen—with gas masks on, bayonets fixed, and rifles locked and loaded with one round of ammunition in the chamber—advanced toward the crowd. Company A was on the right flank, Company C on the left flank, and Troop G in the middle. As guardsmen advanced, they launched more

At 12:05 P.M., the Guard fires tear gas, then advances on the rally. Reprinted with permission of Kent State University Special Collections and Archives.

tear gas into the crowd. Because of the tear gas and the advancing troops, some demonstrators retreated up Blanket Hill between Taylor and Johnson halls; others retreated toward the east between Taylor and Prentice halls, ending in the Prentice Hall parking lot. Some of the students retreated inside the buildings to avoid the tear gas and to put water on their faces. Many in the area left. Once the guardsmen neared the Victory Bell, they split into two groups. Company C, commanded by Maj. Harry Jones, went up Blanket Hill toward the Prentice side of Taylor Hall and held the ground between Taylor and Prentice halls. Troop G and Company A, commanded by General Canterbury and Lieutenant Colonel Fassinger, followed the majority of demonstrators up Blanket Hill between Taylor and Johnson halls.[89]

After advancing, Company C held a line between Taylor and Prentice halls that prevented any demonstrators from returning to the Commons through that corridor. Company A and Troop G, however, upon reaching the top of Blanket Hill near the Pagoda (the highest elevation of land), proceeded down the other side of Taylor Hall toward the Practice Field rather than simply remaining in place to block reentry to the Commons. The students in the area split to let the guardsmen pass, some moving down the hill toward Lake and Olson halls and others going toward the Prentice Hall parking lot to the southeast of Taylor Hall. However, when some demonstrators found themselves on the Practice Field, the guardsmen who were marching toward

Students exit the Commons as guardsmen advance. Photo copyright John P. Filo. Reprinted with permission.

it slowed down to give these students time to escape through the small opening in the fence. This took some demonstrators to Midway Drive and a gravel parking lot near Dunbar Hall.[90] Most students left the area entirely, however. At this point, the assembly on the Commons was disbanded and the Guard's mission accomplished.

Company A and Troop G advanced down the reverse slope of Blanket Hill past Taylor Hall, across the access road, and then onto the Practice Field. Along the field's far side was a six-foot, chain-link fence, capped with barbed wire, that formed a cul-de-sac for the advancing troops. According to the *Report of the President's Commission*, "The feeling had spread among students that they were being harassed as a group, that state and civic officials had united against them, and that the university had either cooperated or acquiesced in their suppression. They reacted to the guardsmen's march with substantial solidarity," shouting epithets at the troops. The guardsmen, for their part, "generally felt that the students, who had disobeyed numerous orders to disperse, were clearly in the wrong." Moreover, they saw the burned remains of the ROTC building as evidence of the destruction the students could cause.[91]

The *Report of the President's Commission* indicates that the crowd split at this time. Some of the more vocal demonstrators ended up in the Prentice Hall parking lot, but most students spread along the balcony of Taylor Hall or onto the hill south of Taylor Hall overlooking the Practice Field and above the access road.[92] Both the Justice Department's Summary and the *Report of the President's Commission* concluded

The Guard advances past Taylor Hall to the Practice Field. Members of Troop G kneel and aim at vocal demonstrators in the Prentice Hall parking lot. Photo copyright John P. Filo. Reprinted with permission.

that while the guardsmen were on the Practice Field, demonstrators threw rocks at them; both reports also speculated that a nearby construction site near Dunbar Hall provided rocks and stones to throw. Guardsmen then threw tear gas canisters at the demonstrators in the parking lot and toward those standing on the hill below Taylor Hall; some threw rocks as well. Students retaliated by lobbing some canisters back at the Guard, prompting cheers from the onlookers on the hill near Taylor Hall. One account described this exchange of projectiles by students and guardsmen as a "tennis match."[93] The distance between the guardsmen and the students made many of the rocks ineffective, although four guardsmen claimed they were hit with rocks at this time.[94] "The distances between the mass of the students and the Guards were later stepped off by expert judges, who concluded that students would have required good right arms like Mickey Mantle's to have reached the guardsmen with even small stones."[95]

During a ten-minute stay on the Practice Field, some members of Troop G were ordered to kneel and point their rifles toward the demonstrators as a gesture of force.[96] The demonstrators in the Prentice Hall parking lot, directly in the line of fire of the kneeling guardsmen, were between 150 and 200 feet away.[97] Student Alan Canfora, who would later be shot, went inside the practice fence and waved a black flag to protest the Guard's actions. Although both the Justice Department's Summary and the *Report of the President's Commission* concluded that this was the time that the

Guard was receiving the most verbal and physical insults, guardsmen aimed their rifles but did not shoot in self-defense. Later they would claim self-defense as the reason for shooting from Blanket Hill. Major Jones, who had accompanied Captain Snyder and the members of Company C to the Prentice side of Taylor Hall to block access to the Commons, "walked through the crowd to find out if General Canterbury wanted assistance."[98] Based on the ease with which Jones passed through the crowd, Davies concluded: "If the demonstrators were as dangerous as Canterbury claimed after the killings, could a solitary officer have elbowed his way through them without some kind of incident? Yet that is exactly what happened."[99]

At the time that Major Jones was on the Practice Field, there was a huddle of the Guard leadership, prompting some to speculate that it was at this time that tactics were developed that included firing directly on the demonstrators. While Michener concluded that there was not an order to fire shared at this time, he added, "It seems likely, however, that on the football field, when the students were being obnoxious and stones were drifting in, that some of the troops agreed among themselves, 'We've taken about enough of this crap. If they don't stop pretty soon we're going to let them have it.'" He further concluded, "It seems likely that some kind of rough verbal agreement had been reached among the troops when they clustered on the practice field."[100]

According to the *Report of the President's Commission*, General Canterbury realized that there was nothing more his troops could do on the Practice Field, so he ordered them to retrace their steps up Blanket Hill and then back down to the remains of the ROTC building on the far side of the Commons. "My purpose," Canterbury explained, "was to make it clear beyond any doubt to the mob that our posture was now defensive and that we were clearly returning to the Commons, thus reducing the possibility of injury to either soldiers or students."[101] There was some speculation that the troops spent all of their tear gas while on the Practice Field and had left none for the return march to the ROTC building. This was not the case. "Both Captain Srp and Lieutenant Stevenson of Troop G were aware that a limited supply of tear gas remained and Srp ordered one canister loaded for use at the crest of Blanket Hill."[102] General Canterbury and Major Jones both claimed under oath that the guardsmen spent all of their tear gas canisters while on the Practice Field. As they marched back up Blanket Hill, they assumed a common V-shaped formation, perhaps to accommodate the terrain of the land. According to Davies, a sequence of photographs used in the trials illustrated that members of Troop G appeared to lag behind the others and seemed to be more concerned with the demonstrators in the parking lot, rather than those who appear in the photographs to be closer to them and to the other troops. Photographs show guardsmen other than members of Troop G looking forward as they advance up the hill.[103]

On seeing what they perceived as a retreat of the Guard, some students felt that everything was over. Several followed behind the Guard at a distance of sixty feet or greater. An eight-millimeter film by student Christopher Abell shows that:

As guardsmen march from the Practice Field to the top of Blanket Hill at the Pagoda, students think that the troops are returning to their station on the Commons. Photo copyright John P. Filo. Reprinted with permission.

A member of Troop G, looking over his shoulder and down toward the parking lot, would have seen five students at a distance of 60 to 85 feet, 25 students between 85 and 175 feet, and 30 students between 175 and 325 feet. . . .

The evidence of the film is that at no time before Troop G opened fire were they being approached by more than 17 students, that none of the approaching students was closer than 85 feet, and that 10 of them were more than 175 feet away. . . .

The film provides conclusive evidence that the guardsmen had not been rushed. [104]

As the Guard marched up the hill, the crowd ahead parted to let them by. Some demonstrators threw rocks at them as they marched up the hill toward the Pagoda. However, rocks were not thrown at the time of the shooting. [105]

As the Guard approached the Pagoda around 12:24 P.M., apparently en route to the ROTC building straight ahead down the slope, guardsmen on the trailing edge of the right flank, mostly from Troop G, wheeled 135 degrees to the right to face the direction of the Prentice Hall parking lot. By all eyewitness accounts and photographic evidence, these guardsmen turned in unison, lifted their rifles in unison, pointed their

At 12:24 P.M., the line of Guard unexpectedly wheels 135 degrees. During thirteen seconds, twenty-eight of the seventy-six guardsmen on the hill fire sixty-seven shots toward the Prentice Hall parking lot. Photo copyright John A. Darnell. Reprinted with permission.

weapons, and began shooting for thirteen seconds, spending sixty-seven rounds.[106] After the firing had begun, Lieutenant Colonel Fassinger, Major Jones, and General Canterbury yelled, "Cease Fire!" Major Jones hit several men on the helmet to stop their firing.[107] Students dove for cover during the thirteen seconds of gunfire—some unsuccessfully.

Four Kent State students were killed. William Schroeder, a nineteen-year-old psychology major and member of the ROTC, was shot in the back at the seventh rib while lying prone 390 feet from the firing position. Sandra Scheuer, a twenty-year-old speech pathology and audiology major, was shot in the front side of her neck on her way to a speech therapy class. She also was 390 feet away from the line of fire. Jeffrey Miller, a twenty-year-old psychology major, was shot in the mouth while facing the Guard 265 feet away. Allison Krause, a nineteen-year-old Honors College art major, was diving for cover in the Prentice Hall parking lot when she was shot. She was 343 feet away from the line of guardsmen as a bullet passed through her left upper arm.

Nine Kent State students were wounded. Joseph Lewis (60 feet away) was shot twice, in the right abdomen and the left lower leg. He was closest to the Guard among the wounded students, on a sidewalk near Taylor Hall. John Cleary (110 feet away), who fell near the Solar Totem sculpture in front of Taylor Hall, was shot in the left upper chest. Thomas Grace (200 feet away) was shot in the left ankle. Alan Canfora (225 feet away) was shot in the right wrist as he dove for cover behind a tree. Dean Kahler (300 feet away) was shot in the left side of the small of his back while lying prone on the ground near the access road. He was permanently paralyzed by the bullet. Douglas Wrentmore (329 feet away) was wounded in the right knee. James Russell (375 feet away) was the only person wounded who was outside the angle of the gunfire leading to the parking lot. He was standing near the Memorial Gymnasium, around 90 degrees from the other students, when he was wounded in the head and right thigh by birdshot. Robert Stamps (495 feet away) was shot in the right buttock. The wounded student farthest from the Guard, D. Scott MacKenzie (750 feet away) was shot in the left rear of the neck.[108] All of those shot on KSU's campus on May 4, 1970, were students of the university. They were not outside agitators or SDS Weathermen. Michener, Mayer, and syndicated columnist Victor Riesel (reported in Davies) have suggested or stated that outside agitators were to blame for much of what happened on May 4, 1970.[109] However, other sources reject the validity of this conclusion.[110] No disruptive outsiders have been identified as participating in the demonstration on May 4.

While sources vary slightly in their accounting, Kelner and Munves place "72 armed guardsmen on the top of the hill" at the time of the shooting. According to the *Report of the President's Commission*, "Twenty-eight guardsmen have acknowledged firing from Blanket Hill. Of these, 25 fired 55 shots from rifles, two fired five shots from .45 caliber pistols, and one fired a single blast from a shotgun."[111] General Canterbury, Lieutenant Colonel Fassinger, and Major Jones all claimed to hear a nonmilitary shot which triggered the rest of the volley. The Justice Department's Summary concluded, "The FBI has conducted an extensive search and has found nothing to indicate that any person other than a Guardsman fired a weapon."[112]

Terry Strubbe, a student at Kent State, set his tape recorder on his dorm window on the first floor of Johnson Hall and left for the rally at noon on the Commons nearby. In 1974, the U.S. Department of Justice paid for an analysis of that tape recording by engineering firm Bolt, Beranek, and Newman of Cambridge, Massachusetts. The report indicated that the first three shots came from M-1 rifles that were located between the Pagoda and the corner of Taylor Hall. It also established that sixty-seven shots were fired, not sixty-one as previously reported.[113] Reexamination of a copy of the Strubbe tape by audio analysts Stuart Allen and Tom Owen in 2010 suggested a verbal order to fire was given before the volley of shots.[114] This agrees with the claims of some students and guardsmen who say they heard an order to fire.[115]

The shooting was done primarily by members of Troop G and Company A, along with two members of Company C who got separated from their company and went with the main body of troops to the Practice Field and back up Blanket Hill.[116] The shooting began with no announcement or warning to the students and no immediate provocation. Some guardsmen claimed they fired because their lives were in danger. However, the Justice Department's Summary noted first that "six Guardsmen, including two sergeants and Captain Srp of Troop G stated pointedly that the lives of the members of the Guard were not in danger and that it was not a shooting situation" and second that "the claim by the National Guard that their lives were endangered by the students was fabricated subsequent to the event."[117] Furthermore, the FBI concluded that students had neither surrounded the guardsmen nor were throwing rocks at the time of the shootings, as some guardsmen alleged. The *Report of the President's Commission* concluded that the "indiscriminate firing of rifles into a crowd of students and the deaths that followed were unnecessary, unwarranted, and inexcusable."[118]

After the thirteen seconds of gunfire, an eerie silence fell. As students lay wounded and dying on the ground, members from Troop G and Company A turned and marched back to the site of the ROTC building, unimpeded by either the hundreds of students on Blanket Hill on the north side of Taylor Hall or observers on the Student Activities Center roof between Stopher and Johnson halls to the west of the Commons.

Company C, which held its position on the other side of Taylor Hall near Prentice Hall to the east, did not fire during those thirteen seconds. Following the shootings, Capt. James Ronald Snyder took seven of his men to assess the conditions of the students wounded in the parking lot. He reportedly looked at two young men and concluded they were dead. Jeffrey Miller had died instantly, but William Schroeder

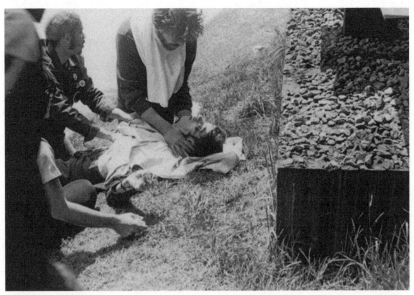

Students are left on their own to care for their wounded classmates. Photo copyright John A. Darnell. Reprinted with permission.

lived for some time after reaching the hospital. Several of Snyder's men were near the body of Jeff Miller when some angry students, having just witnessed the slaughter of their fellow classmates by the other guardsmen, yelled obscenities at them. One of the guardsmen threw a tear gas pellet at the student group in response.[119] The members of Company C returned to their skirmish line and eventually back to the Commons. Captain Snyder later would tell a federal grand jury that he found a pistol and brass knuckles on Jeff Miller's body, although he finally admitted that he concocted this account as a self-defense story for the group of guardsmen in case of legal action.[120]

The students who had witnessed the horrors of the shootings were now left on their own to care for their fellow classmates, who lay dead, dying, and wounded in the Prentice Hall parking lot and on the ground surrounding Taylor Hall. Some ran into the nearby dorms of Prentice and Dunbar halls to call for ambulances and to find help; some went into Taylor Hall to seek out telephones and to find assistance from those inside. Others linked arms around the dead and wounded or administered first aid to those who could still be helped. Still others were frozen in place, unable to respond to what they had just witnessed, or running to the Commons, screaming for ambulances that had not yet arrived. Faculty marshal Glenn W. Frank, a popular geology faculty member, rode with an ambulance from the Commons and assisted in getting the dead and wounded into the ambulances.

As some students helped with the dead and wounded, others began to gather on the hill above the Commons. After ambulances took many of the dead and wounded to hospitals, shocked students began milling around in a daze, eventually joining the other students at the Victory Bell on the Commons. Although the students did not realize it, the potential for another slaughter was extremely high at this time. The *Report of the President's Commission* estimated the crowd that reconvened on the Commons was between two hundred and three hundred. The National Guard stood at one end of the Commons while the students clustered near the Victory Bell. In response to orders from the Guard, students moved away from the Victory Bell to a grassy slope along the edge of the Commons, near Stopher and Johnson halls, where they staged a sit-in. Some expressed anger; others were quiet with shock. General Canterbury and Major Jones were still determined to disperse the crowd. According to the *Report of the President's Commission,* Glenn Frank persuaded General Canterbury to give the faculty marshals some time to try to disperse the students, to avoid any further military action by the Guard. Frank, along with psychology professor Seymour Baron, political science professor Mike Lunine, and history graduate student Steve Sharoff, tried to get the students to leave the site.[121]

James Michener provides the most detailed account of this standoff between the Guard and the students following the shootings.[122] He focuses particularly on the efforts of Professors Frank, Lunine, and Baron to avert more bloodshed. Michener reports that a tape recorder captured a voice from the crowd asking: "Are we going to have any kind of retaliation?" Baron argued that there should be no retaliation, asserting that guardsmen who shot and killed the students were "going to sweat blood." At this point, Baron went to the line of guardsmen and asked who was in charge. When an officer pointed to General Canterbury, Baron approached him and pleaded with him to prevent further action by the Guard. Canterbury reportedly brushed him aside, growling, "Take this man away." A captain took Baron by his arm, escorting him away, but when Baron asked the captain to release him so he could return to the student group to help, the captain replied, "Good Luck."[123]

When Baron returned to talk with the crowd of students, he had little luck in getting them to disperse and go to their dorms or homes; the students were as steadfast as the Guard. Michener reports the students saying: "If they kill us all, let them do it now." Baron ran back to General Canterbury with the hope of averting additional violence, pleading with Canterbury, "'You've got to give those kids some kind of sign.' Canterbury asked, 'Sign of what?' and Baron said, 'That you're not going to shoot. That we can quieten [*sic*] this thing down. Isn't there some kind of order, like 'parade rest'?" Guardsmen, hearing the words "parade rest," reportedly dropped their guns from their shoulders, but Canterbury ordered them to shoulder them again and they responded to his orders. Again Baron pleaded, "'General, can't you make them stop pointing those guns as if they were going to fire?' General Canterbury reflected, looked at the massed students, and said, 'Parade rest.'"[124]

Baron went back to the students and pleaded with them to realize that they were dealing with a general and troops with guns they were willing to use again. "Now if you walk down toward them," he warned, "I promise you they'll kill you. Now the reason they'll kill you is because they're scared to death.... There is only one way you're going to stay alive, and that is to stay here. I don't want you going down there."[125] Someone from the crowd asked, "Who ordered them to shoot?" and Baron replied that he didn't know.

The faculty members again sent a representative to the Guard. This time Mike Lunine ran down toward the Guard in search of General Canterbury. Lunine pleaded that there must be no more shooting. Canterbury did not reply. According to Michener, two university personnel standing with the Guard stated, "'Those students shouldn't be on that hill. There has to be a line drawn somewhere. We've got to have law and order.'" Upon hearing this, Lunine ran back to those on the hill and warned them of what might happen if they didn't move. Lunine returned to the Guard and once again begged the Guard not to shoot, and again one of the university personnel said, "'Professor Lunine, the National Guard does not negotiate under siege.'" Lunine asked whom they were talking about, and the official pointed to the students on the hill. This frightened him deeply and he went back to the students again and pleaded, "'Students, the imminence of slaughter is great.'"[126] A taped exchange makes clear the severity of the situation:

Baron: I'm scared to death that somebody else is going to get shot and killed.

Voice: Man, you take Martin Luther King. He wouldn't be scared.

Baron: Martin Luther King would not have stayed. Martin Luther King was a man who understood that to win you must live. If you die, you cannot win anything. You must live to win. I don't want you kids to die. That won't win you kids peanuts.

Voice: Let them splatter us right now.

Baron: There are too many of you who are too damned good to die in this stinking field here.[127]

After this exchange, graduate student Steve Sharoff approached the Guard. He pointed to his faculty marshal armband and stated that he wanted to speak with General Canterbury. When the Guard led him to Canterbury, Sharoff told the general that the students on the hill would not be moved. The general told him to get them out of there. Sharoff replied that they had just seen four of their friends killed. "'I have my orders,'" Canterbury replied. "'They have got to go.'" When Sharoff tried to argue, Canterbury repeated the same phrase again. It was at this point that Sharoff realized that both groups were determined to hold their ground, and a horrific outcome was imminent.[128]

Glenn Frank was the next faculty member to try to talk with General Canterbury. On his way to the Guard position, he was met by a group of guardsmen led by Major Jones. Frank thought that Major Jones was moving his men out to confront the students. According to Michener, Frank pleaded, "'For God's sake, don't come any closer.' Jones replied, 'My orders are to move ahead,' and Frank said quietly, 'Over my dead body.'" Jones did not move forward. Approaching Canterbury, who was talking with Capt. Ron Snyder, Frank pleaded with the general to give him and the others more time to move the students off the hill. Michener was told that the general said, "They're going to have to find out what law and order is all about." The general told Frank he had five minutes to move the students out; however, Major Manly, who commanded the 181 members of the Ohio State Highway Patrol now on the Commons, effectively told Frank to take all the time he needed.[129] Additional troops were now massing on Blanket Hill above the Commons, effectively surrounding the student sit-in on the hill. Frank approached the students fully convinced of the severity of the situation. A tape from a radio station recorded yelling, threats, cursing, and general noise, followed by Frank's desperate plea:

Voice (over the mob): Here's Glenn Frank.

Voice (over the mob): Hold on, hold on. Wait a minute. Hold it.

Frank (with deep, choking emotion): I don't care whether you've never listened to anyone before in your lives. I am begging you right now. If

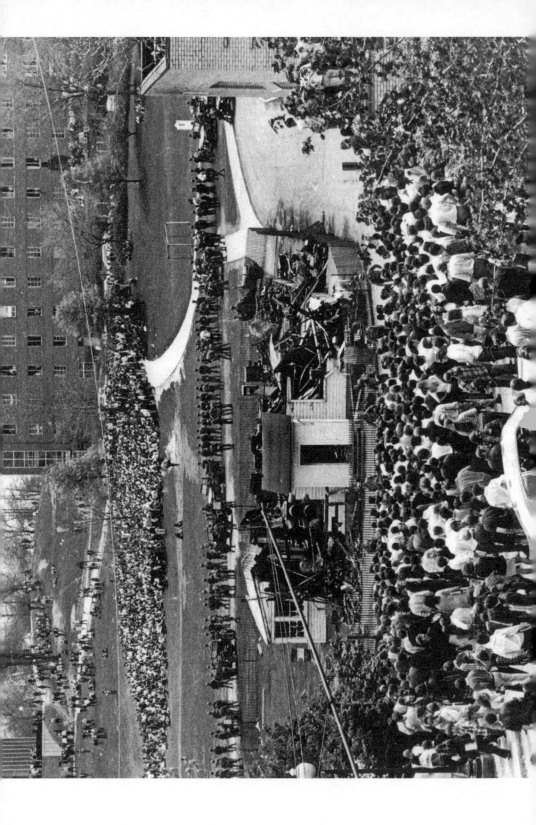

you don't disperse right now, they're going to move in, and it can only be a slaughter. Would you please listen to me? Jesus Christ, I don't want to be a part of this.[130]

Frank's final plea succeeded. By 1:30 P.M., the Commons and the surrounding area were cleared.[131]

The university president, Dr. White, having returned from his lunch at the Brown Derby restaurant, ordered the university closed for the rest of the week as of 1:20 P.M. In addition, Judge Albert L. Caris of the Common Pleas Court of Portage County signed an order granting the injunction request of Portage County's prosecutor, Ronald J. Kane, to close the university until "conditions merit the reopening."[132] Because they were forced to evacuate immediately and could not make arrangements for their departure, students in the dorms left without many of their belongings. At 1:00 P.M., Kent Bell Telephone had shut down phone service to the dormitories, so that students could neither make nor receive calls. "Most of them [were] without access to transportation," as well. "David Ambler, dean for student residence life, had the . . . idea of wheeling out the thirty-six university buses, loading them with students, and starting them off to Cleveland or Columbus, from which spots frantic students could catch what airplanes were available" or otherwise make their way home as best they could.[133] All traffic in and out of the city of Kent was stopped by roadblocks, obstructing parents' efforts to retrieve their children from campus and others from entering or leaving the city. Military personnel patrolled the city and campus and enforced a dusk to dawn curfew.[134]

AFTERMATH

On May 13, the court order closing the university was modified, permitting some personnel access to the university. Because the spring quarter was not over, many faculty corresponded with students by U.S. mail or held courses in their homes or at off-campus sites so that Kent State students could complete the quarter. On June 13, 1970, 1,250 seniors and graduate students returned to Kent State to take part in commencement ceremonies. On June 15, 1970, the court injunction was lifted.[135]

Facing page: Students stage a sit-in near Stopher-Johnson dormitories to protest the shootings. Faculty marshal Glenn Frank convinces students to leave to avoid further tragedy. Photo copyright Don Roese, *Akron Beacon Journal.* Reprinted with permission.

In response to President Nixon's April 30, 1970, announcement of the expansion of the Vietnam War into Cambodia, students throughout the country protested at more than 130 colleges and universities. In response to the shootings at Kent State, that number increased tenfold, resulting in the largest national student strike in U.S. history. The Urban Research team concluded in its 1970 report *On Strike . . . Shut It Down!*: "In spite of Cambodia, without the Kent State deaths, there would have been no national student strike."[136] The Carnegie Commission on Higher Education corroborated in 1971: "With the Kent State shootings, a powerful, emotional response added new fuel and great numbers to the growing turmoil. . . . Throughout the uprising there was exhilaration from doing something personally significant, taking control of events, achieving solidarity and community." In all, 4,350,000 students at more than half of the 2551 colleges and universities in the country participated in the national student strike.[137]

Among the colleges protesting the war and the Kent State shootings was Jackson State College in Mississippi.[138] At Jackson State, as at Kent State, authorities fired indiscriminately at unarmed and unwarned student demonstrators. In 28 seconds, 75 state police shot 150 rounds, primarily aiming at a women's dormitory. They wounded 12 Jackson State students and killed Jackson State student Phillip Gibbs and high school student James Green, who was passing by on his way home from work.[139] As at Kent State, the cause of the shootings has not yet been determined.

For millions of students, faculty, and staff at the nation's colleges and universities during that month in May, the idea of carrying on business as usual on campus was not an option. Fifty-seven percent of university and college presidents reported that their institutions experienced "significant impact" on their campus operations as a result of Cambodia, Kent State, and Jackson State.[140]

Across the nation, the shootings at Kent State changed Americans' consciousness about the Vietnam War. It was the first war to reach into American homes via television.[141] Every evening on the network news, families would hear the body count for that day—as the sight of one of that day's stretchers being lifted into a helicopter emblematized the day's losses. On May 4, 1970, the pervasive image changed to John Filo's instantly iconic photograph of Mary Vecchio kneeling and calling out over the body of Jeffrey Miller, who lay dead on the pavement at Kent State University. Well-known playwright Arthur Miller pronounced in popular *McCall's* magazine: "The war finally came home that day in May when American troops killed our children on their school grounds."[142] A watershed event, the shootings further galvanized Americans' view that the war should end. May 4, 1970, would be written in history through the decades to follow as the day the war came home.

Antiwar sentiment in Congress translated into action. Senator George McGovern, who the day before the Cambodia invasion proposed an amendment to end the war, argued for the amendment's passage by reminding the Senators how deeply the deaths at Kent State had entered the hearts and minds of Americans: "I thank God this amendment was submitted when it was, because as every Senator knows, in the turbulent days following the invasion of Cambodia and the tragedy at Kent State University, this amendment gave a constructive rallying point to millions of anguished citizens across this war-weary land." McGovern then admonished his peers as "partly responsible for sending 50,000 young Americans to an early grave" and charged, "This chamber reeks of blood."[143]

McGovern's address generated substantial support, but not passage, of the amendment to end the war. Congress, however, did begin immediately the withdrawal of funding for the war—a process that continued until the war was brought to an end.[144] Congress took further action by pushing through legislation to lower the voting age to 18. Since World War II, when the age of the military draft was lowered to 18, young people had been arguing, "old enough to fight, old enough to vote."[145] As the number of students demonstrating against the shooting of unarmed demonstrators at Kent State rose into the millions, both Congress and President Nixon desired public action that would respond to the concerns of the college-aged. Within six weeks of the shootings, the president signed a bill lowering the voting age to 18.[146] The Senate unanimously approved the resulting Constitutional amendment, followed by strong support in the House and record-setting quick approval by the states.[147]

The Kent State shootings brought additional legal progress, as the states reformed their tactics for dealing with civil disturbances. When Ohio National Guardsmen moved onto the Kent State campus, the Guard's O-Plan was out of compliance with U.S. Army regulations for dealing with civil unrest. The U.S. Army Field Manual specified that using loaded weapons to control such disorders "is never justified except in the case of armed resistance that trained sniper teams are unable to handle."[148] As the President's Commission on Campus Unrest noted, "This was not the case at Kent State, yet each guardsman carried a loaded M-1 rifle."[149] Although the Commission was appointed by a president opposed to student dissenters, it declared that "the Kent State tragedy must mark the last time that, as a matter of course, loaded rifles are issued to guardsmen confronting student demonstrators."[150] Responding to this recommendation, the Ohio National Guard announced in October 1970 that it would carry nonlethal weapons for campus disturbances.[151] Forty-six other states notified the U.S. Department of Defense that they, too, would follow this regulation.[152]

The legal aftermath of the killing and wounding of Kent State students extended to setting precedent in the U.S. Supreme Court. Initially, the doctrine of sovereign immunity prevented the families from suing members of the Ohio National Guard and other government officials.[153] According to sovereign immunity, members of the government cannot commit legal wrong when acting in their official capacity.

In their 1974 lawsuit, Scheuer v. Rhodes, the families won an appeal to the U.S. Supreme Court when Chief Justice Warren Burger reversed two previous lower court rulings in a landmark reinterpretation of the Eleventh Amendment. The decision determined that sovereign immunity may not be used to block a trial.[154] While the way was cleared for parents of the dead and the wounded students to seek damages, five more years of litigation would end with no one being held responsible for the deaths and injuries resulting from the shootings on May 4, 1970. Thus ended the ten-year legal aftermath of May 4, "one the longest, costliest, and most complex set of courtroom struggles in American history."[155]

The history of the shootings continues to remind us today of the importance of protecting the First Amendment and affirms that, as the father of slain student Allison Krause said, dissent is not a crime. The First Amendment declares our rights to freedom of speech and assembly and to petition our government for a redress of grievances. When the country is at war—within itself or without—those rights become vulnerable.

The President's Commission opens its report with an address "To the American People": "This crisis has roots in divisions of American society as deep as any since the Civil War. The divisions are reflected in violent acts and harsh rhetoric."[156] Neighbors were pitted against neighbors, children against parents, students against officials. Divisive rhetoric further alienated one group from another. The U.S. president called antiwar protestors "bums."[157] The Ohio governor labeled demonstrators in the city of Kent as "worse than the 'Brown Shirt' [sic] and the communist element and also the 'night-riders' and Vigilantes . . . the worst type of people that we harbor in America."[158] Guard officers were in the room to hear Rhodes's speech; guardsmen heard it over the radio. Students who headed for the rally on May 4, 1970, consciously thought they were exercising their First Amendment rights. They did not leave when ordered to do so and shouted "pigs off campus" to guardsmen. Students felt the Guard was violating those rights. Arthur Krause, who lost his daughter Allison to a guardsman's bullet, replied to the nation's president: "She resented being called a bum because she disagreed with someone else's opinion. She felt the war in Cambodia was wrong. Is this dissent a crime? Is this a reason for killing her? Have we come to such a state in this country that a young girl has to be shot because she disagrees deeply with the actions of her government?"[159] Also appealing directly to the president, government, law enforcement, and students, for civil discourse, members of the President's Commission on Campus Unrest conclude, "The very motto of our nation calls for both unity and diversity: from many, one. Out of our divisions, we must now recreate understanding and respect for those different from ourselves."[160]

Notes

1. Richard M. Nixon, "Cambodia: A Difficult Decision," *Vital Speeches of the Day* 36, no. 15 (1970): 450–52.

2. Joe Eszterhas and Michael D. Roberts, *Thirteen Seconds: Confrontation at Kent State* (New York: Dodd, Mead, and Co., 1970), 25.

3. Peter Davies, *The Truth About Kent State: A Challenge to the American Conscience* (New York: Farrar, Straus, and Giroux, 1973), 12; Seymour M. Lipset, "Polls and Protests," *Foreign Affairs* 49, no. 3 (1971): 549.

4. "Tragedy in Our Midst—A Special Report," *Akron Beacon Journal*, May 24, 1970.

5. Davies, *Truth About Kent State*, 12.

6. For "The Justice Department's Summary of FBI Reports" see I. F. Stone, *Killings at Kent State: How Murder Went Unpunished* (New York: Vintage Books, 1970), 60–101: 62.

7. "Tragedy in Our Midst."

8. James Best, "The Tragic Weekend of May 1 to 4, 1970," in *Kent State and May 4th: A Social Science Perspective*, ed., Thomas R. Hensley and Jerry M. Lewis, 3rd ed. (Kent, Ohio: Kent State University Press, 2010), 9; "Tragedy in Our Midst."

9. Davies, *Truth About Kent State*, 13; *The Report of the President's Commission on Campus Unrest* (Washington, D.C.: GPO, 1970), 241.

10. *Report of the President's Commission*, 241; Stone, *Killings at Kent State*, 63; Best, "Tragic Weekend," 10.

11. *Report of the President's Commission*, 241.

12. Davies, *Truth About Kent State*, 13.

13. See, for example, James Michener, *Kent State: What Happened and Why* (New York: Random House, 1971), 125.

14. "Tragedy in Our Midst."

15. *Report of the President's Commission*, 241.

16. Stone, *Killings at Kent State*, 63.

17. Davies, *Truth About Kent State*, 13.

18. *Report of the President's Commission*, 241; Stone, *Killings at Kent State*, 64.

19. Davies, *Truth About Kent State*, 14.

20. *Report of the President's Commission*, 242.

21. Best, "Tragic Weekend," 11; Michener, *Kent State: What Happened*, 131–35.

22. "Struggle to Recovery," *Kent* 3, no. 6 (1970): 4.

23. Stone, *Killings at Kent State*, 64; Best, "Tragic Weekend," 10; *Report of the President's Commission*, 242.

24. Best, "Tragic Weekend," 11.

25. *Report of the President's Commission*, 242–43.

26. Eszterhas and Roberts, *Thirteen Seconds*, 46.

27. "Tragedy in Our Midst."

28. Best, "Tragic Weekend," 12; *Report of the President's Commission*, 245.

29. Charles Fassinger, interview by Carole A. Barbato and Laura L. Davis, Apr. 1, 2007.

30. *Report of the President's Commission*, 246–47; Stone, *Killings at Kent State*, 65.

31. Davies, *Truth About Kent State*, 17; *Report of the President's Commission*, 245.

32. *Report of the President's Commission*, 244; Davies, *Truth About Kent State*, 16.

33. Best, "Tragic Weekend," 13.

34. Stone, *Killings at Kent State*, 66; Best, "Tragic Weekend," 14.

35. *Report of the President's Commission*, 247.

36. "Struggle to Recovery," 5.

37. Best, "Tragic Weekend," 13; Davies, *Truth About Kent State*, 16–17; *Report of the President's Commission*, 248.

38. *Report of the President's Commission*, 248.

39. Stone, *Killings at Kent State*, 66.

40. *Report of the President's Commission*, 249; Stone, *Killings at Kent State*, 66–67.

41. Stone, *Killings at Kent State*, 67; Best, "Tragic Weekend," 14; *Report of the President's Commission*, 250.

42. "Struggle to Recovery," 5; *Report of the President's Commission*, 249.

43. Best, "Tragic Weekend," 14; Stone, *Killings at Kent State*, 67; *Report of the President's Commission*, 249; Davies, *Truth About Kent State*, 18.

44. Stone, *Killings at Kent State*, 67.

45. Jerry M. Lewis, personal communication with the authors, Feb. 5, 2008; *Report of the President's Commission*, 250; Stone, *Killings at Kent State*, 68.

46. Best, "Tragic Weekend," 15; Stone, *Killings at Kent State*, 68.

47. Scott L. Bills, "Introduction: The Past in the Present," in *Kent State/May 4: Echoes Through a Decade*, ed. Scott L. Bills (Kent, Ohio: Kent State University Press, 1988), 13; Davies, *Truth About Kent State*, 17; Peter Davies, "The Burning Question: A Government Cover-up?" in Bills, *Kent State/May 4*, 151; Charles A. Thomas, "Chapter 4: The Burning Question," in *Blood of Isaac*, Charles Thomas Papers, 1970–2003, box 64s, series 10, May 4 Collection, Special Collections and Archives, Kent State University Libraries, Kent, Ohio, <http://speccoll.library.kent.edu/4may70/IsaacFour.htm>.

48. Stone, *Killings at Kent State*, 68; Davies, *Truth About Kent State*, 18–19.

49. *Report of the President's Commission*, 250.

50. Stone, *Killings at Kent State*, 73.

51. Best, "Tragic Weekend," 16; Stone, *Killings at Kent State*, 69.

52. James A. Rhodes, Rhodes Speech on Campus Disorders in Kent, May 3, 1970—Fire House Speech, Political Science Department, Records, 1970, box 70, folder 27, May 4 Collection.

53. Bills, "Introduction," 13; Joseph Kelner and James Munves, *The Kent State Coverup* (New York: Harper and Row, 1980), 71; "Struggle to Recovery," 5; *Report of the President's Commission*, 254; Davies, *Truth About Kent State*, 22–23, 25.

54. "Struggle to Recovery," 5.

55. "Tragedy in Our Midst"; Davies, *Truth About Kent State*, 22.

56. Best, "Tragic Weekend," 18.

57. Stuart Taylor et al., *Violence at Kent State, May 1 to 4: The Students' Perspective* (New York: College Notes and Texts, 1971), 48.

58. Stone, *Killings at Kent State*, 70–71; Best, "Tragic Weekend," 17.

59. "Tragedy in Our Midst."

60. Stone, *Killings at Kent State*, 71.

61. Stone, *Killings at Kent State*, 71–72; Best, "Tragic Weekend," 17–18; *Report of the President's Commission*, 257–58.

62. Best, "Tragic Weekend," 18; Davies, *Truth About Kent State*, 26–28.

63. Stone, *Killings at Kent State*, 72.

64. "Struggle to Recovery," 6.

65. Davies, *Truth About Kent State*, 28.

66. "Tragedy in Our Midst."

67. Harold M. Mayer, *Commission on KSU Violence*, 4 vols., unpublished report, Kent State University (Kent, Ohio: KSU Printing Service, 1972), 1: 22.

68. Ibid.

69. *Report of the President's Commission*, 259.

70. *Report of the President's Commission*, 260–61; Davies, *Truth About Kent State*, 31.

71. Best, "Tragic Weekend," 19; *Report of the President's Commission*, 260–61.

72. Michener, *Kent State: What Happened*, 324–25.

73. *Report of the President's Commission*, 255.

74. Michener, *Kent State: What Happened*, 325.

75. *Report of the President's Commission*, 261, 263–65.

76. Stone, *Killings at Kent State*, 75.

77. Davies, *Truth About Kent State*, 34; Michener, *Kent State: What Happened*, 329–30.

78. *Report of the President's Commission*, 263.

79. Ibid., 265.

80. Kenneth R. Calkins, "The Frustrations of a Former Activist," in Bills, *Kent State/May 4*, 104.

81. Stone, *Killings at Kent State*, 75; *Report of the President's Commission*, 288.

82. "Struggle to Recovery," 6.

83. "Struggle to Recovery," 6; *Report of the President's Commission*, 263; Stone, *Killings at Kent State*, 76.

84. *Report of the President's Commission*, 264; Stone, *Killings at Kent State*, 77.

85. *Report of the President's Commission*, 265–66; "Tragedy in Our Midst"; Stone, *Killings at Kent State*, 77.

86. Stone, *Killings at Kent State*, 77; *Report of the President's Commission*, 267.

87. Stone, *Killings at Kent State*, 78.

88. Michener, *Kent State: What Happened*, 331; and James Ronald Snyder, whose testimony provided the same account, transcript of *Arthur Krause et al. v. James A. Rhodes et al.*, District Court of the United States for the Northern District of Ohio Eastern Division, 1975, vol. 20, p. 4751, May 4 Collection.

89. Stone, *Killings at Kent State*, 78–79.

90. Ibid., 79–80; Davies, *Truth About Kent State*, 34; *Report of the President's Commission*, 266–67.

91. Michener, *Kent State: What Happened*, 337; *Report of the President's Commission*, 266–67.

92. *Report of the President's Commission*, 267.

93. Stone, *Killings at Kent State*, 81; *Report of the President's Commission*, 267.

94. Stone, *Killings at Kent State*, 81.

95. Michener, *Kent State: What Happened*, 336.

96. *Report of the President's Commission*, 268; Stone, *Killings at Kent State*, 81–82; Kelner and Munves, *Kent State Coverup*, 139.

97. Davies, *Truth About Kent State*, 41.

98. Stone, *Killings at Kent State*, 82; *Report of the President's Commission*, 267.

99. Davies, *Truth About Kent State*, 38–39.

100. Davies, *Truth About Kent State*, 41–42; Michener, *Kent State: What Happened*, 361, 409–10.

101. *Report of the President's Commission*, 268.

102. Stone, *Killings at Kent State*, 82.

103. Davies, *Truth About Kent State*, 42.

104. Kelner and Munves, *Kent State Coverup*, 174–75; *Report of the President's Commission*, 270.

105. *Report of the President's Commission*, 270–71; Stone, *Killings at Kent State*, 87.

106. Davies, *Truth About Kent State*, 45; Kelner and Munves, *Kent State Coverup*, 177; Michener, *Kent State: What Happened*, 340.

107. Best, "Tragic Weekend," 25; *Report of the President's Commission*, 272.

108. Davies, *Truth About Kent State*, 52–55; *Report of the President's Commission*, 273–76.

109. Michener, *Kent State: What Happened*, 352, 409, 411; Mayer, *Commission on KSU Violence*, 4: 2–23; Davies, *Truth About Kent State*, 142.

110. Robert M. O'Neil, John P. Morris, and Raymond Mack, *No Heroes, No Villains: New Perspectives on Kent State and Jackson State* (San Francisco, Calif.: Jossey-Bass, 1972), 7; *Report of the President's Commission*, 239; Stone, *Killings at Kent State*, 61; "Tragedy in Our Midst."

111. Kelner and Munves, *Kent State Coverup*, 192; *Report of the President's Commission*, 273.

112. Stone, *Killings at Kent State*, 89.

113. Kelner and Munves, *Kent State Coverup*, 177.

114. John Mangels, "New Analysis of 40-Year-Old Recording of Kent State Shootings Reveals that Ohio Guard Was Given an Order to Prepare to Fire," Cleveland.com, May 9, 2010, <http://blog.cleveland.com/metro/2010/05/new_analysis_of_40-year-old_re.html>.

115. *Report of the President's Commission*, 275.

116. Ibid., 277.

117. Stone, *Killings at Kent State*, 84; Captain Snyder testified that he fabricated the self-defense story for the Guard to use, transcript of *Arthur Krause*, vol. 20, 4850–56.

118. Stone, *Killings at Kent State*, 87; *Report of the President's Commission*, 289.

119. Best, "Tragic Weekend," 25; *Report of the President's Commission*, 277.

120. Kelner and Munves, *Kent State Coverup*, 124–25; Snyder testimony, transcript of *Arthur Krause*, vol. 20, 4850–56.

121. *Report of the President's Commission*, 278.

122. The dialogue in this passage is taken from the interpretive account in Michener, *Kent State: What Happened*, 400–08. Michener wrote the dialogue after listening to a tape recording.

123. Michener, *Kent State: What Happened*, 401–02.

124. Ibid., 402.

125. Ibid., 404.

126. Ibid., 404, 405.

127. Ibid., 405.

128. Ibid., 405, 406.

129. Ibid., 406.

130. Michener, *Kent State: What Happened*, 407; *Report of the President's Commission*, 278.

131. Best, "Tragic Weekend," 24.

132. *Report of the President's Commission*, 285–86; "Struggle to Recovery," 11.

133. Michener, *Kent State: What Happened*, 419–20.

134. "Struggle to Recovery," 11.

135. Ibid., 19.

136. *On Strike . . . Shut It Down! A Report on the First National Student Strike in U.S. History, May 1970* (Chicago, Ill.: Urban Research Corporation, 1970), 1.

137. Richard E. Peterson and John A. Bilorusky, *May 1970: The Campus Aftermath of Cambodia and Kent State* (Berkeley, California, 1971), xi, 1, 3; Kirkpatrick Sale, *SDS* (New York: Vintage Books, 1974), 635.

138. Christina Kukuk, "The Gibbs-Green Affair," *The Burr* (2000): 8–13.

139. *Report on the President's Commission*, 289, 462, 430–32.

140. Peterson and Bilorusky, *May 1970*, 15.

141. Michael Mandelbaum, Vietnam: The Television War, <http://www.jstor.org/stable/10.2307/20024822>, 157.

142. Arthur Miller, "The War Between Young and Old, or Why Willy Loman Can't Understand What's Happening," *McCall's*, July 1970, 32.

143. Senator George McGovern, speaking for the amendment to end the war, on Sept. 1, 1970, to the Senate, 91st Cong., 2nd sess., Congressional Record 116, pt 23:30682.

144. Mitchell K. Hall, *The Vietnam War*, rev. 2nd ed. (New York: Pearson Longman, 2008), 64.

145. Pamela S. Karlan, "Ballots and Bullets: The Exceptional History of the Right to Vote," Stanford Public Law and Legal Theory Research. Research Paper No. 45 (December 2002): 16–17 <http://papers.ssrn.com/sol3/papers.cfm?abstract_id=354702>.

146. Jack Rosenthal, "'65 Act Extended, 11 Million More Would Be Allowed to Ballot in All Elections," *New York Times*, June 23, 1970.

147. Title 3, The President, 40th Anniversary of the 26th Amendment, by the President of the United States of America, *The Federal Register/FIND* 76, no. 131 (July 8, 2011): 40215.

148. *Report of the President's Commission*, 289.

149. Ibid.

150. Ibid., 290.

151. "National Guard to Carry Non-lethal Weapons," *Daily Kent Stater*, Oct. 7, 1970.

152. Davies, *Truth About Kent State*, 169.

153. For a detailed discussion of the court cases and investigations related to the May 4 shootings, see Thomas R. Hensley, "The May 4th Trials," in Hensley and Lewis, *Kent State and May 4th*, 64–86.

154. Scheuer v. Rhodes, 416 U.S., 232 (1974), <http://caselaw.lp.findlaw.com/cgi-bin/getcase.pl?court=us&vol=416&invol=232>.

155. Hensley, "May 4th Trials," 64.

156. *Report of the President's Commission*, 1.

157. Juan de Onis, "Nixon Put 'Bums' Label on Some College Radicals," *New York Times*, May 2, 1970.

158. Rhodes, Speech.

159. In *The 20th Century with Mike Wallace: The Legacy of Kent State* (documentary), prod. Janis Klein, CBS News/The History Channel, 1996; VHS tape, The History Channel, 2000.

160. *Report of the President's Commission*, 6.

For Further Information

Visit the Kent State University May 4 Visitors Center
101 Taylor Hall

Visitors entering the May 4 Visitors Center seek answers to their questions about the shootings and reflect on the meaning of May 4th today by experiencing three galleries. The first gallery establishes the backdrop of the 1960s, which saw tremendous strain and change. The second gallery immerses the visitor in what happened on May 4th—at a rally typical for the times, but ending quite differently. Visitors see and hear the differing memories and perspectives related to the event, while understanding that there are well-documented facts. The third gallery shows the breadth and the depth of the impact of May 4th, from military reform to affirming the importance of protecting the First Amendment. Throughout, visitors of all generations understand that young people can make a difference in the course of history. Visitors conclude their experience of the exhibit with opportunity to record their responses.

Follow the May 4 Walking Tour

Outdoors, trace the steps of history within the May 4 site, placed on the National Register of Historic Places in 2010. Pick up a map brochure from the stand across from the entrance to the May 4 Visitors Center in 101 Taylor Hall. Add to your experience by checking out an iPod to play the Walking Tour documentary, *May 4, 1970: Someone to Tell the Story*. The tour ends at the May 4 Memorial, a place for quiet reflection.

The May 4 Collection and website (http://www.library.kent.edu/page/11247) assist students, faculty, staff, community members, and other researchers in locating information sources about the Kent State shootings and their aftermath.

FOR ADDITIONAL INFORMATION

For additional information about May 4-related resources and events, go to www.kent.edu/may4.

Join us on Facebook 🄵 and Twitter 🄱.

Recommended Reading and Viewing

Barbato, Carole A. "'Embracing their memories': Accounts of Loss and May 4, 1970." *Journal of Loss and Trauma* 8 (2003): 73–98.

———, and Laura L. Davis, eds. *Democratic Narrative, Memory and History*. Kent, Ohio: Kent State Univ. Press, 2012.

Bills, Scott L., ed. *Kent State/May 4: Echoes Through a Decade*. Kent, Ohio: Kent State Univ. Press, 1988.

Casale, Ottavio M., and Louis Paskoff. *The Kent Affair: Documents and Interpretations*. New York: Houghton Mifflin, 1971.

Confrontation at Kent State (documentary film). Directed by Richard Myers. CAK Fund, 1970. VHS tape, Kent State University, 1981.

Davies, Peter. *The Truth About Kent State: A Challenge to the American Conscience*. New York: Farrah, Straus, and Giroux, 1973.

Erenrich, Susie, ed. "Kent and Jackson State: 1970–1990." Special issue, *Vietnam Generation* 2, no.2 (1990).

Fire in the Heartland: Kent State, May 4, and Student Protest in America (documentary film). Directed by Daniel Miller. Fire River Productions, 2010.

Grace, Thomas M. "Kent State: The Struggle for Memory and Meaning." *The Sixties: A Journal of History, Politics and Culture* 2, no. 2 (2009): 245–49.

———. *Kent State: Death and Dissent During the Long Sixties, 1958–1973*. Amherst, Mass.: Univ. of Massachusetts Press, forthcoming.

Hensley, Thomas R. *The Kent State Incident: Impact of Judicial Process on Public Attitudes*. Westport, Conn.: Greenwood Press, 1981.

Hensley, Thomas R., and Jerry M. Lewis. *Kent State and May 4th: A Social Science Perspective*. 3rd ed. Kent, Ohio: Kent State Univ. Press, 2010.

Jedick, Peter. *Hippies*. 1998. Berkeley: Creative Arts Books: 2001. Electronic book, Kindle, 2011, Nook, 2011.

Kelner, Joseph, and James Munves. *The Kent State Coverup*. New York: Harper and Row, 1980.

Morrison, Joan, and Robert K. Morrison, eds. *From Camelot to Kent State: The Sixties Experience in the Words of Those Who Lived It*. New York: Times Books, 1987.

On Strike . . . Shut It Down! A Report on the First National Student Strike in U.S. History, May 1970. Chicago, Ill.: Urban Research Corporation, 1970.

Smith, Karen Manners, and Tim Koster, eds. *Time It Was: American Stories from the Sixties and Beyond.* Upper Saddle River, N.J.: Pearson Prentice Hall, 2007.

The Report of the President's Commission on Campus Unrest. Washington, D.C.: GPO, 1970.

Stone, I. F. *The Killings at Kent State: How Murder Went Unpunished.* New York: Vintage Books, 1970.

Taylor, Stuart, et al. *Violence at Kent State, May 1 to 4, 1970: The Students' Perspective.* New York: College Notes and Texts, 1971.

The 20th Century with Mike Wallace: The Legacy of Kent State (documentary). Produced by Janis Klein. CBS News/The History Channel, 1996. VHS tape, The History Channel, 2000.

The Day the War Came Home (documentary film). Directed by Chris Triffo. Partners in Motion/Single Spark Pictures, 2000. DVD, Single Spark Pictures, 2010.

What Is the Meaning of May 4 for Today?

The shootings at Kent State on May 4, 1970

- spurred the largest national student strike in U.S. history;
- changed Americans' consciousness about the Vietnam War;
- encouraged Congress to respond to the concerns of young people, including lowering the voting age to 18 and beginning to withdraw funding for the war;
- changed Ohio National Guard regulations so that nonlethal weapons were carried for campus disturbances;
- set a precedent in the U.S. Supreme Court, allowing public officials acting in the capacity of their office to be brought to trial for their actions;
- remind us of the importance of protecting the rights of the First Amendment;
- show us the need to communicate effectively and respect differences;
- demonstrate that young people can make a difference.

About the Authors

Carole A. Barbato is professor of communication studies and Laura L. Davis is professor of English and faculty coordinator for May 4 initiatives, both at Kent State University. Barbato was a friend of Sandy Scheuer and Bill Schroeder and Davis was a witness to the shootings. For more than a decade, they have taught the Kent State course "May 4, 1970 and Its Aftermath." Local experts, commentators, and authors on the subject of May 4, their published work includes the first-person experience account "Ordinary Lives" in *Time It Was: American Stories from the Sixties and Beyond* and editorship of the essay collection *Democratic Narrative, History, and Memory* (Kent State Unievrsity Press, 2012). They are cocreators of the Kent State University May 4 Visitors Center and May 4 Walking Tour and in 2011 received a $300,000 grant from the National Endowment for the Humanities to support fabrication of the permanent visitors center exhibit. Barbato, Davis, and Mark F. Seeman, Kent State University archaeologist and professor of anthropology, along with Kent State sociology professor Jerry M. Lewis, coauthored the nomination to place the site on the National Register of Historic Places. Seeman's long-term interest in the preservation of cultural resources has included membership on the Ohio Historic Site Preservation Advisory Board. In 2010 Seeman led the nomination project to a successful conclusion for the fortieth commemoration of May 4.